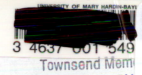

From Rubble
to Rejoicing

222.806
J17f

From Rubble to Rejoicing

A Study in *Effective Christian Leadership Based on Nehemiah*

by Donald Jacobs

WILLIAM CAREY LIBRARY
Pasadena, California

Published by
William Carey Library
P.O. Box 40129
Pasadena, California 91114
(818) 798-0819

LC# 91-65000
ISBN 0-87808-213-1

The New International Version of the Bible is used
throughout this work unless otherwise indicated.

Printed in the United States of America

Contents

v

Social Disciplines

Management Disciplines

Introduction
Why Nehemiah?

A grandmother sat on her rocking chair mending clothes, sewing a patch here, stitching a tear there, when the grandchild who was playing at her feet looked up at her and asked, "Grandma, what does God do all day?" Pausing for a moment to collect her thoughts Grandma replied, "God spends all of his time fixing things that are broken." It is a full-time job!

As we read the Scriptures we see the Spirit of the Lord at work taking impossible situations and, through persistent effort, putting the pieces together with great care and pain. Of course, the enemy is there to bring it all to destruction, and so the drama goes on—the enemy destroying, the Lord repairing. But then Jesus turns the tables on the enemy. He invades Satan's kingdom and brings him down. "The reason the Son of God appeared was to destroy the works of the devil" (I John 3:8). In turn, Jesus Christ takes that which has been wounded by the devil and creates wholeness. He finds rubble and, through his marvelous grace, turns that rubble into strong walls. From rubble to rejoicing, that is the way God works. Out of chaos he created the marvelously

ordered universe, the world we now inhabit with
gratitude.

Christian leaders are hard at work doing what God
does. They confront the devil who is intent on wrecking
all that God has done and in the name and power of
Jesus Christ they lead the church in this cosmic warfare.
This task is extremely demanding because leaders do not
lead from behind, but they are the first to lead the charge
against the devil and his hosts. In so doing they rally all
believers to take heart and do battle bravely. Christian
leaders serve an absolutely crucial role in the work of
God.

Perhaps you are one of these leaders. Take heart, God
provides a special anointing which enables the leaders
he calls to do marvelous things. Leaders are astonished
by what God can do through them if they only believe,
obey and give him the glory.

During the final hours before his crucifixion, Jesus
turned to his disciples—those who would give leadership to his church—and said, "I tell you the truth. Anyone who has faith in me will do what I have been doing.
He will do even greater things than these because I am
going to the Father. And I will do whatever you ask in
my name, so that the Son may bring glory to the Father.
You may ask me for anything in my name; and I will do
it" (John 14:12-14). That promise stands today. So while
Christian leadership is an awesome responsibility, it is
also the most exhilarating vocation imaginable because
in a very special way God energizes and enables his appointed leaders to do the "greater things."

Now and again a Christian leader does well to sit back
and examine once again his or her role in the plan of
God and to ask whether the enabling of the Lord continues to supply all needs. That is the purpose of this little study. As you read it and as you honestly answer the
questions and ponder anew God's call in your life, do

open your heart to God's renewing grace. He did not call you to strive to do his work in your own power and wisdom. He called you as a willing partner in the greatest ministry ever assigned to a person, the opportunity of working with God to reconcile the world to himself. My prayer for you is that "you may be filled to the measure of all the fullness of God" (Ephesians 3:19).

What Biblical leader should we concentrate our attention on? There are so many. They pass before us: Abraham, David, Ezekiel, Peter, Paul, and the list goes on. Each is worthy of study. But I have chosen to study the life of the leader of Israel when the curtain fell on the Old Testament story: Nehemiah, the governor of Judah under King Artaxerxes.

I chose him for several reasons. Not, by the way, because he had no faults. He had plenty of problems and weaknesses. But because he was called by God to help Israel in one of its most desperate hours. Nehemiah responded and led God's people from a state of confusion and despair to a new era of hope and joy in the Lord, from rubble to rejoicing.

Situations such as Nehemiah faced are much like the situations many of us face. Walls are down; Doors are burnt. Things are in a bit of a mess. Maybe former leaders allowed things to deteriorate, and now you are left with the rubble. Perhaps the group is split and is full of hostility and bitterness. Or maybe the people are just plain worn out, dry and lifeless. These situations are ready made for miracles of grace.

Also Nehemiah lived at a time of social upheaval in Israel. Old certainties were being questioned; a generation was confused and without a sense of direction. Nehemiah who was himself a child of two cultures knew something of the trauma of social displacement. Many leaders in the newer churches of the world face crises like this.

Let us then examine Nehemiah from every angle. Let us see him as a human being, just as we are; but let us also learn from him how to open ourselves to the mighty power of God who wants to reconcile all things unto himself.

In this study we will attempt to find principles of Christian leadership which can be applied in any culture in the world. The Bible does not elevate one style of leadership above all others; there is no "Democratic" style, no "Presbyterian" or "Episcopal" way that is pointed out as superior. All of these styles can be found, to some extent, in Scripture. In fact, God employed many different styles of leadership to lead his people. Moses, for example, did not lead in the same manner as the Apostle John, nor did King David lead like John the Baptist. Each leader had a style appropriate to his or her time, and each reflected the personality of the leader.

Each leader is unique and cannot be duplicated. However, there is a common characteristic among all Christian leaders: they carry in their hearts the living presence of the Lord Jesus Christ who is the Way, the Truth and the Life. Jesus is so alive in them that their leadership is a showcase where God's grace in Jesus Christ is on display for all to see. So even though the styles of leadership change through the ages and from culture to culture, the common factor is the abiding presence of Jesus Christ in the ministries of all. That is the single characteristic which sets them apart from all worldly leaders. They exhibit in life the character of Jesus Christ.

Colossal social changes are overtaking many Christian congregations around the world. Sometimes Christians in the West are distressed with the social change that they see around them. But when compared to many churches in what is called "the Third World," the pace of change in the West is ponderously slow. The churches in Tanzania where I had the privilege of serving for a dozen years are living in the midst of unbelievably rapid social change. It is as though someone pushed the "fast forward" button on the tape player, and everything is speeded up. Leading people at a time of such great change requires a special portion of God's stabilizing grace.

Added to these problems is the additional fact that many of the leaders in the newer churches have inherited leadership positions from "missionaries" who often exercised an "alien" style of leadership. Local leaders are expected to simply carry on without changing the structure. For some, it is like David trying to wear Saul's armor; it simply does not fit. Leadership patterns and styles must be culturally authentic and must "fit" the leaders; if not, everyone suffers. Forms and patterns are, I reiterate, optional. But Christian leadership principles are not; they are essential. So we will concentrate our attention not so much on one's leadership style as on what is in the heart of the leader.

The study of Nehemiah which follows can be used for personal reading and study, or it can be used as a textbook for teaching groups. To facilitate its usage, each chapter has a scripture text at the beginning and study questions at the end. Do not race through these study questions, but ponder them with prayer and self-examination.

PART I

God's View of Leaders

Leadership:
A Gift to the Church

*It was he who gave some to be apostles . . .
prophets . . . evangelists . . . pastors . . .
teachers, to prepare God's people for works of
service, so that the body of Christ may be built
up . . . attaining to the whole measure of the
fullness of Christ.*
—Ephesians 4:11-13

Even before he laid the foundation of the world, the
Creator God planned that his people would need and
should have leaders. He purposed that leaders be an
essential part of his great plan to bring the message of
the Gospel to every people on earth and to form fellowships of faith in which Jesus Christ has the preemi-
nence. God has done and is doing his part. But he can
only do so through leaders. Anywhere in the world that
leaders truly lead in the spirit of Jesus Christ, people
move forward. Where leaders are not taking their God-
appointed positions, the people, unfortunately, suffer.

3

People are not created like bees who have instincts either to lead or to follow, having no choice in the matter, simply acting as their genes dictate. Babies are not born with labels, "This one is a leader." We are created with leadership potential, but that potential must be released.

We sometimes speak of "born leaders." Are they "born" that way or is it a spiritual gift which is given by the laying on of hands? Both are correct. The potential must be there to begin with. And when that potential is called out and affirmed by the fellowship of God's peo-ple, symbolized by the laying on of hands, then the circle is complete. Both potential and calling are necessary.

We know that God has planted leaders in our congre-gations. The question is, who are they? How can they be identified? Furthermore, how can they be encouraged and enabled to take their rightful places among God's people? How are they to be equipped for their demand-ing tasks? These are the questions facing the church around the world. Identifying, calling out and training leaders is one of the most important issues facing God's people today. Jesus recognized this fact and he encoura-ges us: "Ask the Lord of the harvest, therefore, to send out workers into his harvest field" (Matthew 9:38). It would be consistent with the Scriptures if we paraphrase this prayer, "Pray that he will send forth leaders."

Think About It!

Why are leaders so important in the life of God's people? Since believers in Christ have the presence of the Holy Spirit so that each person is, in a sense, enligh-tened, what is the purpose of leadership? How much difference does a good, effective leader make in nurtur-ing the people of God?

2

Jesus Christ: Our Example

Fix your thoughts on Jesus, the apostle and high priest whom we confess.

—Hebrews 3:1

Have you ever thought about how fortunate we are to have in the Bible stories about a great variety of leaders? In fact, when God tells the story of his involvement with Israel, he does so by telling about each leader in succession. The history of Israel is the story of her leaders. This should not surprise us because God normally leads his people by giving them gifted and empowered leaders. How else could he possibly lead his people? He has chosen this way. The Bible tells of some leaders who were very effective, such as Moses, and some who were not, like King Saul. The Scripture hides nothing.

Even the subject of this study, the Prophet Nehemiah, was not without glaring faults. He got so angry on one occasion that he quite lost his head. Hear his own words,

"I contended with them and cursed then and pulled out their hair" (Nehemiah 13:25). This behavior would not be appropriate in a Christian congregation today anywhere in the world. So Nehemiah cannot be elevated to a sinless eminence, nor can any of us. However, when all is said and done, we can learn much from the life of this great man. But we must always concentrate on the principles rather than the forms of leadership.

Even though many leaders appear in the Bible, they all pale in significance when compared to Jesus Christ of Nazareth. He is God in human form, the perfected leader. Therefore his leadership remains the standard. So, even though this study will not concentrate on Jesus' leadership specifically, all that is said should be weighed on the balance of Jesus' own leadership model and must be judged against his life-changing teaching.

Think About It

Some people think that Jesus Christ was so "special," so different from us, that we cannot possibly attain to his style of leadership. Do you think that is true? What is there in Jesus' leadership style which is the most difficult for you to follow? By what authority did Jesus lead?

3

Nehemiah:
An Effective Leader

"If it pleases the king . . . let him send me to the city in Judah where my fathers are buried so that I can rebuild it."

—Nehemiah 2:5

The Bible is so rich in stories of great leaders that it is difficult to choose one among the many to study. But if we ask what leaders excelled in a time of desperate need and at a time when God's people faced overwhelming problems, Nehemiah comes quickly to mind. You will recall that he was mightily used of God to build Jerusalem's broken walls and then to participate in an extraordinary revival which brought Israel to repentance. He walked into a confused, homeless situation, but with God's spirit enabling him he brought beauty out of the ashes.

Who was Nehemiah? He was a Jew who suddenly appeared as a great man in the court of King Artaxerxes of Babylon. When the Babylonians destroyed the once mighty Jerusalem in 588 B.C. they took away into Babylon some of the Jews as slaves. Nehemiah's great grandparents were probably among them. Approximately a hundred years of exile had passed before Nehemiah was born.

For several generations Nehemiah's forefathers taught and lived their faith in the midst of a hostile culture. It was into this family that Nehemiah was born. He was reared in a Jewish ghetto in the capital of the great Babylonian Empire. So at one and the same time his religious convictions were formed in his home and among his people while he was also educated in the advanced learning of the Babylonians.

The Scriptures do not tell us how it happened that this young Jewish man was brought into the service of the great King Artaxerxes. Presumably he "rose through the ranks." Certainly many local Babylonians aspired to this position, but King Artaxerxes saw in Nehemiah unmistakable leadership characteristics. This fine Jewish man was both qualified and trustworthy. Hence, Nehemiah found himself in a high position in the Babylonian court.

As noted earlier, Nehemiah participated in both the Persian and Jewish cultures, a fact which made him an outstanding person. He knew Persian science, philosophy and language. He ate Persian food, read Persian books; he was fully at home in the Persian culture. Nevertheless, he learned at the feet of his father Hachaliah, a devout Jewish father. The center of his life was undoubtedly his relationship with God and his covenant people, Israel. Never for a moment did he sell out his faith in order to join fully the society of Persia whose religion was idolatrous. It is not easy to be separate from the world while living every day in that culture. But Nehemiah kept his eyes on Jehovah God and was therefore able to be a Jew in Persian dress.

Often godly leaders are people who appreciate more than their own cultural tradition. Many Christian leaders today stand, as it were, in the gap between different cultural groups. They are called upon to use their total learnings and experience for the sake of the Gospel. In the early church, Barnabas and Saul were such leaders. They were at home in both Greek and Jewish cultures. The church owes much to leaders who can bridge cultures for the sake of Christ. Nehemiah was such a person in his day.

Many Christian leaders find themselves in the center of storms caused by social change. Perhaps the reader is one of them. As things change all around us we often ask, "Is it possible to do any good in these rapidly changing circumstances?" A study of Nehemiah will convince us of the fact that it is possible if God is in it, and if we are obedient. It is not easy to stand with one foot in the past, another in the present, all the while keeping one's eyes in the future. But that is what Christian leaders are called upon to do.

Think About It

Many leaders in newer churches relate to people who have been Christians for a long time and who have developed a "Christian lifestyle." On the other hand, they also relate to people who have come to faith in Jesus Christ more recently. All are wrestling with how Christians should live in their context. Those who have been Christians longer may try to dictate how Christians should live their lives. Those new to the faith may resist such regimentation. What is the leader's responsibility to help these two kinds of people listen to one another? How important is strong leadership as people are converted and brought into the community of faith?

Sometimes churches are divided over secondary issues. What is the role of a leader in this kind of situation?

4

Nehemiah's Preparation

I was cupbearer to the king.

—Nehemiah 1:11

When the story opens, we find Nehemiah in charge of the wine of King Artaxerxes in Shushan, Babylon's royal city. What was the role of the cupbearer in the Persian court? First of all, trustworthy cupbearers made sure that no poison got into the wine (poisoning was a favorite way, in those days, of disposing of kings). The king had to trust him, so cupbearers were chosen with great care. They had to be incorruptible because the temptation to take bribes to " do a job" was not unheard of. The king relied on his cupbearer completely. For this reason cupbearers were usually also in charge of the king's purse.

Josephus, the historian, wrote that Nehemiah was second in command under the Persian king. History bears this out. He wielded awesome power in that far-flung Persian empire. How he rose to such a position of prominence as a "foreigner" sounds more like a

11

fictional novel than a historical record. But God does marvelous things for the sake of his people.

As one of Artaxerxes' right-hand men, Nehemiah had access to the good things of the land. He had more fame, wealth and comforts in his "foreign" home than many of the local Babylonians had. As a respected leader in the king's court he had achieved a certain status. As far as Nehemiah was concerned, he had reached the top. Only the king was above him. Hundreds and thousands were under his authority. What more could he want?

We are reminded of an earlier leader of Israel, Moses, who also had at his disposal the wealth, power and position of a magnificent nation, Egypt. Like Nehemiah he felt the heavy weight of God's call, so he turned his back on his privileges and took upon himself the rigors of leading God's people. "He chose to be mistreated along with the people of God . . . He regarded disgrace for the sake of Christ as of greater value than the treasures of Egypt" (Hebrews 11:25, 26). Both Moses and Nehemiah point to Jesus who "being in very nature God, did not consider equality with God something to be grasped, but made himself nothing, taking the very nature of a servant, being made in human likeness. And being found in appearance as a man, he humbled himself and became obedient to death, even death on a cross" (Philippians 2:6-8).

It is true, Nehemiah could have enjoyed the pleasures of the Persian royal court for the rest of his life. And that may have been the story of his life if it were not for the fact that he carried in his heart the knowledge of the God of Abraham, Isaac, Jacob, of Moses and Joshua, of David and Elijah. This knowledge of God was no doubt planted in Nehemiah's soul by his remarkable father Hachaliah, and by his unnamed mother who fed her precocious son not only food prepared by faithful Jewish hands but food for the soul which formed in

Nehemiah's inner man a burning desire to serve the God who long ago had rescued his people from Egypt with the strong hand of salvation.

God's people could never forget that their God was a Savior God. He desired for his people freedom from bondage. While serving in the King's court, that fire burned but dimly in Nehemiah's heart, yet it never went out. It was put there by God himself. A time would come when this smoldering fire would leap into flame, not only radically changing Nehemiah's personal life but also affecting the lives of God's people, Israel, in a dramatic fashion.

His duties in the royal court, however, required all his energies, so Nehemiah gave himself wholeheartedly to the service of the splendid king Artaxerxes without giving much thought to his own people who were, after all, hundreds of miles away.

As far as we know, Nehemiah carried no bitterness in his heart toward the Persian people or the Persian government of which he was a part, even though the Persians had earlier invaded and plundered Jerusalem and all Judah, leaving them in tatters. Rather, he did his work diligently and with integrity. Things were going well. He had an exalted position, all the money he could desire, influence beyond his wildest dreams; and he was the pride and joy of both Israel and Persia.

And so it was that as Nehemiah was going about his duties in the Persian court, Hanani, one of his "brothers" (perhaps a distant cousin), together with a few other inhabitants of Jerusalem, appeared one day in Shushan, the capital city of Babylon, to pay Nehemiah a visit.

Whether these men had returned to Jerusalem with Ezra a few years before or were permanent residents in Jerusalem we are not told. Perhaps Nehemiah assumed that when Ezra and his six thousand returnees entered

Jerusalem things would go better. Their return certainly made some difference. But Ezra concentrated his attention on rebuilding the Temple which he was able to do to some degree. He also worked with the holy books and re-established the service of the priests. But Jerusalem still lay in rubble.

Nehemiah asked his visitors how things were in Jerusalem. The answers were uniformly bleak. The walls were broken down, the gates were destroyed and no one seemed to be able to do anything about this unhappy state of affairs. Life in Jerusalem was a tale of misery. The enemies of Jerusalem, such as Sanballat, king of Samaria, raided the holy city any time they wished.

Having told their desperate tale, Hanani and his Jewish friends departed to return to the wounded Jerusalem, and Nehemiah was left with this awesome burden crushing his spirit. How could he enjoy the abundance and the security of Babylon while his own people in Jerusalem were vulnerable to marauders? He gave himself to prayer and fasting for a number of days. During that agonizing time, he realized that God intended that he himself should shoulder the responsibility of going to Jerusalem and of rebuilding those walls which could give the people some sense of security. And that is the heart of the story.

Our study will concentrate on Nehemiah's personal life, the call that came to him, and how he carried out the awesome responsibility which God laid on him. This should help us to understand the principles which all effective Christian leaders must follow if they are to lead people closer to God.

It should be noted here that leadership qualities are found in sisters as well as in brothers. The language through this study will be "he" and "him." This is simply shorthand used for the sake of simplicity. God calls women as well as men to specific responsibilities in his great work of redemption.

Think About It

How important is trustworthiness in a leader? In what areas do leaders sometimes compromise Christian principles and in so doing lose people's trust? What constitutes a "bribe"? Should the church have a higher ethical standard regarding money, sex and power than "ordinary good citizens" have?

Many of the great leaders in the church were called while they were successful in a secular occupation. Their calling required a sacrifice to serve the Lord. Can you cite examples of such people in your fellowship? Does the church actively seek for leaders among such people? Should it?

PART II

Requirements for Effective Christian Leadership

Effectiveness in Christian Leadership can be measured by examining whether the leader is moving the people closer to conformity with God and his Word. Any other criteria for measuring effectiveness must be questioned, such as whether the leader is gaining power, fame, position or wealth. These are irrelevant goals. Jesus keeps warning us that we dare not view leadership as the people of the world do. They have their own criteria for success. Jesus declared that he who would be greatest must be the servant of all.

An effective Christian leader should grow in four areas: in spiritual disciplines, in personal disciplines, in social disciplines, and in management disciplines. As we study Nehemiah, we are impressed with how much he applied himself in each of these areas of his life. He was not perfect by any means, but his example is well worth studying. We will carefully analyze each of these disciplines in Nehemiah's life and use them as mirrors in which to see ourselves.

5

Spiritual Disciplines:
Receiving Vision

I had not told anyone what my God had put in my heart to do for Jerusalem.

—Nehemiah 2:12

I also told them about the gracious hand of my God upon me .

—Nehemiah 2:18

Nehemiah was changed by a vision. He received that vision as he listened to his Judean friends and when he prayed and fasted. No doubt in his mind's eye he saw those ugly broken walls and scorched doors. The scene must have depressed him nightly. But God lifted his eyes above that wreckage and gave him a vision of Jerusalem restored, its walls standing firm and strong, and its people secure and safe in its protection. We do not know exactly how it happened, but Nehemiah caught God's vision, and it changed his life. Every spiritual advance must first be a vision in someone's mind and heart.

It soon came clear to Nehemiah that God now wanted his people to move back to Jerusalem and rebuild it. The exile was over. There was a time to leave Jerusalem and a time to return. Now was the time to return. God-given vision will reveal which way God is moving his people. Nehemiah would have been left high and dry had he stayed in Babylon because God's attention had shifted from preserving his people in Persia to bringing them together to begin again in Jerusalem.

Leaders are in danger of working hard at something which is of only secondary concern to God. They continue, in a sense, to squeeze grapes for Artaxerxes while God is concerned about the restoration of his people in Judah. They miss out on the action because they do not comprehend what God is doing. They need to have an up-to-date vision of what God intends to do.

Nehemiah's vision can be divided into two parts. First, he had a vision of God's overall plan—in this case, to re-establish his people in Israel. Then, secondly, he had to know what to do in order to bring the vision to reality. At some point along the way Nehemiah discovered that God wanted him to supervise the building of Jerusalem's wall. He had a general vision and a specific vision. And so it is with us. We need both visions.

A vision is an insight into what God's will is in a particular situation, and that vision provides a fixed point of reference so that all of one's energies can be directed toward that end.

Vision answers the question, "What is God doing?" Too many people focus on their own self-fulfillment and therefore miss the boat. True Christian leaders do not concentrate on fulfilling self but on fulfilling what God is doing in the world. It is only as they lose themselves in God's vision that they discover the purpose for their own being. When they participate with

God in doing what he wants done, they "find themselves," as Jesus promised. This is the way to have a life of meaning and purpose. Any lesser path will lead to futility and self-hate.

Why does God share his vision with leaders? There are many reasons. Primarily, of course, this is the only way he can get his work done on earth. Then, too, a vision gives focus and meaning to life. When we concentrate all of our energies on a particular project, it is amazing what can be done. Weightlifters amaze us with their phenomenal strength. They can lift those heavy weights because they concentrate all of their energies on that one task. Other people are able to concentrate so intensely that they can stretch themselves upon a bed of spikes. Leaders who concentrate on a task with intense single-mindedness are highly successful.

Then, too, if we have a God given vision we can see further down the road than others. Because of this, we can sustain exceptional efforts for a long period of time. It keeps us from giving up or giving in. That vision undergirds hope and determination. When people falter, the vision pulls us forward.

God's most effective leaders were people who received a vision from the Lord. *Abraham* saw a great new nation in a fruitful land. *Jacob* saw a ladder of blessing joining heaven and earth. *Moses* saw a loving God leading His people out of bondage. *Deborah* saw God's people freed from the Canaanites. *Isaiah* saw the glory of God filling the temple. *Jonah* saw a city full of people doomed if they did not repent. *John the Baptist* saw the Lamb of God coming to him for baptism. *Peter* saw in a vision that God could and would save Gentiles. The *Apostle Paul* often spoke of his vision to reach the Gentile world for Christ. All of these people allowed God to shape them around a compelling vision.

A leader without a God-given vision will lead his people nowhere. "Where there is no vision, the people perish" (Prov. 29:18 A.V.).

Sometimes it happens that leaders receive a great, compelling vision, but somewhere along the way they are unfaithful to it. At that point they are in extreme danger because they may substitute their own vision for God's, thereby producing diabolic confusion.

Jesus took time to commune with his Father and in that way he kept his vision alive. We can do no less than Jesus himself. We must be absolutely sure that the vision is of God and not of ourselves. This is confirmed through prayer and fellowship with God.

While on this point of vision it should be noted that when one particular vision is fulfilled, God often gives another in order to move the work forward. The overall vision remains, but the details of how to move toward the realization of that vision may change from time to time. When the wall was complete, Nehemiah did not simply relax and quit. God gave him a new vision for a new task, to bring spiritual revival to Jerusalem so that people could once again live in harmony with God's purposes. The overall vision remained the same—God's desire to re-establish his people in Israel. Nehemiah's particular vision needed to be constantly updated. And so it is with us.

Think About It

Describe the vision which God has given you. How did you receive that vision? Has that vision been reaffirmed since you first received it? Could you have exercised spiritual leadership without that vision? Have you been faithful in fulfilling the vision? Do you feel that you are simply doing a job or are you fulfilling a compelling vision? Do you need a new particular vision?

6

Spiritual Disciplines:
Walking With God

I sat down and wept. For some days I mourned and fasted and prayed before the God of heaven.

—Nehemiah 1:4

Nehemiah had a relationship with God even when he was the king's cupbearer. He obviously read the Word of God often and meditated on it. In this way he was prepared to comprehend the vision when he received it. His walk with God must have been very meaningful to him. We do not have a detailed description of Nehemiah's devotional life, but it is evident that he had learned how to tarry before the Lord. Out of these times spent alone with God, Nehemiah's mind and heart were shaped and molded.

He did not start his intense devotional life only after he had the vision. On the contrary, it was because he walked closely with God that he could receive the vision in the first place. No doubt he had a meaningful walk

23

with God even before this specific call to help with the reconstruction of Jerusalem.

An effective Christian leader lives in the presence of God continually—so close to God, in fact, that he can hear God's voice and can sense his gracious presence in all circumstances. An effective Christian leader walks with one hand in God's hand and the other reaching out to the people. He brings God and man together. He has an ear toward God and an ear toward mankind. It is only by reading God's Word, by meditating and praying that the purifying light of God can keep the vision clear and paramount. We lose our sense of direction quickly when we neglect our moment-by-moment relationship with God. Like Enoch of old, we must walk with God.

The king noticed the changes that had overcome Nehemiah when his faithful cupbearer returned to his duties after his prolonged stay in God's presence. He was astonished. "Why," he inquired, "does your face look so sad when you are not ill? This can be nothing but sadness of heart" (Neh. 2:2). When our heart rejoices at that which rejoices God's heart and when we are crushed by that which crushes Gods heart, we can be sure that we are truly walking with God.

Think About It

How important to a leader is a fresh, dynamic devotional life? What is the present state of your own devotional life? Have you known leaders who neglected their life of study and devotion even though they had received a call from God and were busy in the Lord's work? What do you determine to do about giving yourself more fully to walking closely with God?

7

Spiritual Disciplines:
Repenting

"Let your ear be attentive, and your eyes open, to hear the prayer your servant is praying before you day and night for your servants, the people Israel. I confess the sins we Israelites, including myself and my father's house, have committed against you. We have not obeyed the commands, decrees and laws you gave your servant Moses."

—Nehemiah 1:6-7

As far as God was concerned, Nehemiah was not prepared to assume leadership among the people of God until he learned the way of repentance. Nehemiah must have surely resisted saying that little sentence, "I have sinned." Who among us is quick to repent? Somehow, deep down, we know that if we do not repent the problem is really not our problem. Yes, we might help a bit here and there, but there is no heartfelt burden. By simply not repenting we can go on our merry way without doing anything about the problem and without ourselves being changed. A person who has a repentant spirit knows that he must change. He also will assume some responsibility for the problem, and that is always costly.

Nehemiah could have insisted that the problems came on Israel because of their persistent disobedience. They should simply accept their predicament as part of God's way of showing his righteousness. "Serves them right," he could have said. "What we are witnessing is simply God's judgement in action, and who would dare try to stop it?"

Or he could have said, "Jerusalem's problems are for the Jews who live in Jerusalem. Let me go on working for Artaxerxes. Maybe some day I will do them a favor when I feel that I can do so without losing any of my honor, prestige, or money."

Or he could have resolved, "These people are stiff-necked. I will pray for them every day. Maybe some day they will learn they cannot play about with God. They are so thick-headed!"

But in the white light of God's holiness Nehemiah saw clearly the stain of sin in his own life. That brought his spirit to repentance. His heart was broken before God. With bitter tears he fell before the cleansing altar, "I confess the sins we Israelites, including myself and my fathers house, have committed against you. We have acted very wickedly toward you. We have not obeyed the commands, decrees and laws you gave your servant Moses" (Neh. 1:6-7). The broken spirit is open to God's word of Grace. Nehemiah heard that word of grace, and he was forgiven.

But the moment Nehemiah repented of his own sin he saw that he, too, was at least partially responsible for Jerusalem's plight. This admission changed the man dramatically. From then on he knew he had to get involved. True repentance not only admits to sin, but a repentant person is prepared to do something about the problem.

Blessed are the leaders of God's flock who can repent. But why do leaders find it hard to repent? Perhaps they feel that people will despise them if they repent. It might be that they have been covering up a sin which repentance will reveal. To repent of that sin, they may reason, will cost them their position or reputation. Or they may simply be deluded into thinking that they have no sin, as described clearly in I John 1. Only weaknesses, personality characteristics and temptations. Leaders can become stubborn and hardened in their attitudes, resulting in their straying further and further from God. They may become very judgmental because they find it hard to forgive in others the sins of which they themselves are guilty.

Sometimes leaders find it hard to repent because they do not really wish to forgive. They punish others by withholding forgiveness, or at least they think that is what they are doing. Leaders who are ready to forgive others are usually those leaders who are repentant themselves.

Jesus was tempted just as we are. Listen to him in the Garden when he pled before his Father. "Father, if you are willing, please take away this cup of horror from me" (Luke 22:42, Living Bible). He was terrified by the prospect of going to the cross. He was tempted to avoid it completely. Maybe he dreaded the possibility that if he were to take on the world's sin, people and spirits would suspect him of being a sinner. He became *sin* for us, not a sinner. It is always a terrifying thing to expose sin. As Jesus did on Calvary. He not only exposed sin in all of its ugliness but also died as the supreme sacrifice to take away sin. He shuddered at the prospect. But in the garden of decision, he submitted to the will of His loving Father, "Not my will, but yours be done" (Luke

22:42). Jesus had no reason to repent because he had no sin, but he showed by his resigned spirit the way to true repentance.

Repentance is practiced first at home. A church leader will probably treat the church the way he treats his wife and his family. Someone said that a leader who is unable to repent is like a vehicle without a reverse gear. Sooner or later it will land the person in an impossible situation.

Think About It

What is the difference, if any, between admitting an error and repenting? Describe a repentant spirit. How can we make it easier for others to repent? Think of your own spirit. Would others point to you as an example of someone who repents quickly? Think about it. What is the relationship between repentance and forgiveness? What do you think about the statement, "Repentance is the oil which keeps relationships running smoothly?"

Spiritual Disciplines:
Praying Effectively

"Let your ear be attentive and your eyes open to hear the prayer your servant is praying before you day and night."

—Nehemiah 1:7

Then I prayed to the God of heaven, and I answered the king .

—Nehemiah 2:4

Nehemiah came to the point where he had to make a decision in Artaxerxes' court. He had a responsibility, as a servant of the king, to do the king's wishes. But God was shaping a vision in Nehemiah's mind which would sooner or later require Nehemiah to go to Jerusalem, away from Artaxerxes' court. Nehemiah must have found this extremely difficult. In order to resolve the issue he gave himself to prayer.

Note the way in which he prayed. In this instance he tarried in prayer. He sat down, he wept, he mourned, he fasted, he prayed before the God of heaven for a number of days. Nehemiah knew the discipline of extended prayer. Many Christian leaders are very conscientious about getting time apart for prayers of intercession and guidance. But for some of us, when we are busy we neglect our prayer life, even though we know that the more responsibility we have, the more we need to pray.

It is in prayer that spiritual battles are fought and won. As we just noticed, Jesus himself wrestled with his desire to drink some other cup in the garden. He fought the battle in prayer. There in the garden when his disciples were asleep he entered into a moment of deep, life changing prayer. When he yielded his spirit to do the Father's will, the way was clear for defeating the enemy. Spiritual battles are fought in the arena of prayer.

Nehemiah also prayed quick, short prayers. When standing before the king he had to come up with an answer on the spot, so he prayed to God and got a quick answer. A Christian leader knows that prayer is his very life support. A Zimbabwean bishop told me what he did when a guerilla pointed a gun at him. "For the first time in my life, I prayed with my eyes open." That was instant prayer!

Nehemiah already knew the power and necessity of prayer, but before too long he discovered that earnest prayer was very costly. It cost him his career and his comfort. We know that when we pray earnestly, we open ourselves to the possibility of getting personally involved. God often involves us in answering our very own prayer.

Nehemiah also understood the context of prayer. Prayers which reach God are based upon a knowledge of the judgment and the mercy of God. This is the context in which all of our praying needs to take place. Secondly, he knew the necessity of self-disclosure. "I have sinned," he pleaded. "I need grace." Thirdly, he knew he could not do God's work without God's enabling. "Prosper the work of your servant," he prayed.

Nehemiah, unlike some of us, did not spend much time telling God what he should do; rather his prayers were specifically to discover what God wanted done so that he could join God in doing his will. This is what praying "in Jesus' name" means; it is the process of seeking to know what *Jesus'* will is. Nehemiah knew this kind of prayer, and that was the central feature of his life.

Think About It

What are some of the conditions for effective prayer? Which are best, long prayers or short ones? Why are the prayers of some people answered while the prayers of others are not? Does more time spent in prayer mean more effectiveness in prayer? If God knows what he wants, then why should we pray to him? Can he not do it anyway? What are the greatest hindrances to prayer? What part should prayer play in the life of a leader?

9

Spiritual Disciplines:
Placing God's Will First

*"O Lord, let your ear be attentive to the prayer
of this your servant and to the prayer of your
servants who delight in revering your name. . . .
I was cupbearer to the king."*

—Nehemiah 1:11

Nehemiah heard God's clear call. God wanted him to assist in the rebuilding of Jerusalem. But he had a responsible position already, and he was successful there. Why change? But God held the question before Nehemiah. "Do you want to do what *you* want to do, or what *I* want to do?" Should he enjoy the good things which were the rewards of his work in the king's court or should he, like Moses, determine "to suffer with the people of God?"

Nehemiah received his answer while praying. He concluded that he had no option; he had to obey God no matter what that would mean to him personally.

Jesus also submitted his will to God's will. "Although he was a son, he learned obedience from what he suf-

33

fered" (Heb. 5:8). We remember his cry in Gethsemane, "If there be some other way . . . Not my will but thine be done."

One of the things which dulls a leader's effectiveness is the tendency to halt between doing what God wants and what he himself wants. We sometimes hear leaders ask, "Where will I get the best salary?" Or, "If I go there, will it be an advancement or a demotion?" Questions such as this skirt the real issue which is, "What does God want?"

Sometimes what God wants and what I want are about the same. There is not much difficulty there. But there are times when I do not want what God wants. That is where the cross appears. When my will crosses God's will, someone must submit to the other. It is at such times that I must die to selfish desires in order to do God's will.

It is very important that leaders analyze their motives regularly lest personal interests slowly intrude into one's ministry and, like weeds, crowd out the good growth.

In summarizing his life, the great apostle Paul said, "I was not disobedient to the vision from heaven" (Acts 26:19). That vision completely rearranged Paul's life. He could no longer do what he wanted to do. He had to find out what God wanted and then do it no matter what it cost him. And we know that obedience to God exacted a high toll for Paul. "Five times I received from the Jews the forty lashes minus one. Three times have I been beaten with rods, once I was stoned, three times I was shipwrecked, I spent a night and a day in the open sea . . . I have labored and toiled and have often gone without sleep; I have known hunger and thirst and have often gone without food. I have been cold and naked" (II Cor. 11:24, 25, 27).

Think About It

What did Paul mean when he wrote, "I die daily" (I Cor. 15:31)? What does it mean to be "in the will of God"? How do you know when you are "in God's will"? How did Nehemiah discover God's plan for his life? Can leaders assume that they will know God's will? How important is it to know what the brothers and sisters think when it comes to discerning God's will?

10

Personal Disciplines:
Growing in Love

"O Lord God of heaven, the great and awesome God, who keeps his covenant of love with those who love him and obey his command."
—Nehemiah 1:5

"Why should my face not look sad, when the city where my fathers are buried lies in ruins, and its gates have been destroyed by fire?"
—Nehemiah 2:3

Divine compassion is the fuel which drives every saint of God. It was his love which motivated God and which bound him with mankind at incalculable cost to himself. It cost him the death of his Son, the highest cost the Father could pay. "God is love," the Scriptures proclaim, and "he who abides in love abides in God, and God abides in him" (I John 4:16). A hallmark of a Christian leader is an indwelling divine love.

In the Greek language, there are three types of love. First there is "eros" which is conjugal love or romantic love. This love operates on the basis of oaths and covenants. It operates within certain obligations and privileges. Then follows "phileo" or brotherly love, the type of love which causes us to love our fellowmen, our clan, those in our club, denomination, race or nation. Even non-Christians have these two types of love; they are not at all uncommon. But there is yet a third kind, "agape" love, which originates in God and which, therefore, loves for God's sake and seeks nothing in return. It is the love which enables us to love those who are, humanly speaking, not deserving of our love—our enemies, so to speak. This is the love which disregards the barriers of language, race, class and nation and insists on loving across barriers which have been painstakingly erected by our society.

This love finds its expression in servanthood. A supreme example of agape was God's desire to wash the feet of his disciples, even though he already knew that one had betrayed him, another would deny him before the rising of the sun, and that all of them would be scattered within a few short hours (John 13). Still, he desired to wash their feet.

The disciples were contentious as that Passover meal began because they wanted to have the question settled: How would the chief offices be allocated in the new Christly government (Luke 22:24-27)? They were so concerned about who was to be the greatest that they had neglected the more urgent question, "Who is the least?"

They badly needed someone to be "least" when they entered that Upper Room because the one who was least was supposed, by custom, to wash everyone else's feet. However, as it turned out no one considered himself the "least," so they ate the most important meal of their lives with dirty feet, a very embarrassing thing to do, especially for ritually pure Jews. Then Jesus showed the way. He took the servant's towel and stooped to wash their feet. He became the "least." This is agape. It is love which walks into another's love with courage and hope.

No doubt Nehemiah had "phileo" in his heart to some extent. He was a Jew and as such was naturally concerned about Jewish welfare. But it was not a love which was compelling enough to cause him to leave his "secular job." "Phileo" does not necessarily require sacrificial action.

The point came, however, when Nehemiah began to love with an extraordinary love, with "agape." Then his heart wept when he thought of the condition of God's people. God put a love in his heart which would burn into a compelling flame. That love for God, for his people and for God's will inspired Nehemiah through the terrible, difficult days which followed. Unwarmed by divine love, a leader's heart will serve only self, or will serve only those who serve him. In the end, all is lost.

How can we demonstrate more fully God's extraordinary love? Where do we fail in this regard? And how can we recapture the life-changing potential of the love with which God in Christ loves us?

A leader whose heart is full of divine love is unconsciously authoritative. He does not take this authority to himself; rather it is bestowed by God and is recognized as authentic by God's people. There is a great difference between authoritative leadership and authoritarian leadership. The authoritative leader serves because he is empowered by God and is therefore supported by the people of god. The authoritarian leader, on the other hand, accumulates power and uses that power to guarantee that his position is preserved and strengthened. Christian leaders must be aware of using God-given gifts in order to stay in the good graces of people or for private or family gain.

Our love is too often controlled by human categories. We love those who will love us in return. The Apostle

Paul prayed a prayer for the Ephesians which would also do us good. He prayed that they would "grasp how wide and how deep is the love of Christ" (Eph 3:18). The arms of Christ's love know no limits. This is "agape," and it is ours in Christ Jesus.

Think About It

It may be helpful to consider the difference between the "kingly" style of leadership and the "servant" style. How does a king get into power? How does he go about discipling his citizens? How are his successors chosen? If a "kingly" type of person becomes a servant leader, will he be deposed? Does the "king" style reproduce servant leaders or more "kings"? How does all of this relate to leadership in the church?

11

Personal Disciplines:
Growing in Knowledge

"Remember the instruction you gave your servant Moses, saying, `If you are unfaithful, I will scatter you among the nations; but if you return to me and obey my commands, then even if your exiled people are at the farthest horizon, I will gather them from there and bring them to the place I have chosen as a dwelling for my Name.'"

—Nehemiah 1:8-9

"So you handed them over to their enemies, who oppressed them. But when they were oppressed they cried out to you. From heaven you heard them, and in your great compassion gave them deliverers, who rescued them from the hand of their enemies."

—Nehemiah 9:27

Nehemiah and Ezra (Nehemiah's colleague) had studied the Scriptures so thoroughly that they comprehended the ways of God in a remarkable way. Chapters 9 and 10 of Nehemiah's book contain a brilliant summary of God's ways of working with Israel. Nehemiah was remarkably conversant with the history of Israel, the conditions of the covenant, the character of God and the other lofty themes of Israel's theology.

You will remember, also, that the first chapter records Nehemiah's prayer in which he recalled the entire story of God's dealing with Israel; furthermore, he perceived that the vision which God had given him was consistent with what he had learned of God through his own study of Scripture.

Many leaders fail to really wrestle with the deepest theological issues facing the people of God. They often go through life with a superficial grasp of Christian theology and are, therefore, unable to meet the challenges of the ever-changing social scene. The writer to the Hebrews laments the fact that many Christians never do grow theologically. They keep talking about superficial issues, never going on to learn the deeper lessons of Christian discipleship (Heb. 6:1-2). They are milk-fed, and if they are leaders they dispense only milk. As good as milk is, it must be accompanied by solid food, or there will be no growth.

A leader must recognize that each cultural or historical situation raises its own set of questions. Leaders are largely responsible for the development of a theology based on the Word of God which is relevant to the local needs and understandings. All theology must be kept up-to-date. The Word of God does not change; but that to which it applies, the culture and society, does change. Therefore, Christian leaders must know and do their theology throughout their entire lifetime.

One of the benefits of searching deeply into God's Word is that in it we discover that God works according to a purpose, with a pattern. Each person's individual vision contributes to the totality of God's plan for his people. It is good for leaders to discern these patterns so they can conform to God's total plan. After Bible school or seminary some leaders simply close their theological minds. As they thought when they left their training, so they continue to think until they die. There is no excuse for this. It is important for us to read Christ-honoring books, to attend seminars and courses where the challenges of the present day are faced, to take time off now and again for additional training if at all feasible.

Christ saw his own life clearly in a theological context. In John 13 we read that Jesus, knowing "that he had come from God and was returning to God" took the position of a servant. He could take the lowly place because he understood the wonderful plan of God in which he was a willing participant.

If we have theological perception, and if we continue to grow in our understandings of the Word of God, we have a context out of which we can minister. The little ups and downs, the setbacks and advances— all will be viewed in the light of God's glorious plan which is to bring all things to himself through Christ. Theological understanding provides us with a context in which we can labor with courage.

Think About It

What ways are available for leaders in your group to continue to grow in knowledge and understanding? Are there better ways to assure that all of the leaders grow in their theological and practical understanding? How much theological education should a pastor have? What are some weaknesses in the way your church goes about the training of leaders?

12

Personal Disciplines:
Growing in Integrity

*Moreover . . . when I was appointed to be their
governor in the land of Judah . . . [for] twelve
years—neither I nor my brothers ate the food
allotted to the governor.*

—Nehemiah 5:14

Nehemiah rose through the ranks at Artaxerxes' court
partially because of his uncompromising honesty and
trustworthiness. Those characteristics undergirded his
work when he moved among the Jews while the wall
was being built. We also find this virtue in Joseph who
was tempted again and again to bend God's principles
for personal gain. He refused point blank to do so. Moses
also was entrusted with a colossal responsibility because
he was honest and trustworthy. Ananias and Sapphira,
on the other hand, are examples of warning to all
believers because they were not entirely honest.

In fact every effective Christian leader stands firmly
on the virtue of integrity. Paul wrote, "Stand firm then,
with the belt of truth buckled around your waist" (Eph.

6:14). A military belt was the item of armor which supported all of the other body armor. If integrity is missing in a leader's armor, no amount of cleverness or hard work will make up for that lack. The enemy will finally bring him down.

Down through history, there have been those Christians (notably the Anabaptists) who have refused to take the oath in court. They asked, "Does taking the oath mean that outside of court one does not need to tell the truth?" For a Christian there is no option; he must tell the truth at all times. Christians are always under oath.

Christian leaders must beware of the temptations to be dishonest in three basic areas: in making promises, in financial matters, and in sexual morality. When we make promises, we must try diligently to keep them. Sometimes leaders make promises without the least desire to fulfill them just to please someone or to get out of a tight situation. This should be avoided.

In financial matters leaders must be above reproach. It is wise for pastors to avoid handling or making decisions about church funds. They should never mix church funds with personal funds. Furthermore, they should see to it that all income and expenditures are reported to the people who give. The pastor should never borrow from church funds unless authorized to do so by congregational or district leaders. Even then it is a questionable practice.

In sexual matters, a Christian leader must live above reproach. He cannot be too careful in this area. Especially in counselling or in traveling, a Christian leader must at all times be aware of the traps put there by the enemy. There may be no compromise, even for a minute, in the area of moral integrity. A Christian leader has no privileges in morality. He must be even more circumspect than others. Love of money and sexual impropriety have been the downfall of many gifted Christian leaders.

Think About It

What are some of the greatest temptations in being responsible for church money? Does unwise use of church funds militate against increasing giving? How does that happen? What are some good ways to make sure that leaders will not be compromised in financial matters? At what point is the giving or receiving of a bribe a sin? How openly should the subject of money be discussed in a church? Does one person's indebtedness affect the brothers and sisters in the fellowship? How? Is the church responsible for handling funds or should the pastor do that? What are some guidelines that leaders should adhere to in the area of moral purity?

13

Personal Disciplines:
Growing in Skills

I set a time. . . . "May I have letters to the governors . . . so that they will provide me safe-conduct. . . . May I have a letter to Asaph, keeper of the king's forest . . . ?"
—Nehemiah 2:6-8

It is possible that, having received a vision, a leader stumbles because he simply cannot implement the vision. We sometimes say of a leader, "He has good ideas, but he cannot put them into shoe leather." A friend once said, "I had a good idea, but it didn't work." I humbly reminded the person that part of an idea being good is its workability. If it doesn't work, it probably is not a "good" idea. A vision is essential, but it is also important that the vision be brought into reality by planning and hard work.

Nehemiah had the vision. The walls of Jerusalem were to be built. But walls are not built by good intentions; they are built with plans, people, money, and hard work.

Nehemiah knew this and therefore was prepared with a plan. When the king asked him how long he wanted to be on leave, Nehemiah set a time; he had already thought through that part of the plan. Nehemiah was also ready to tell the king what he needed in order to be successful in his mission. He needed letters which would guarantee him safe passage to Jerusalem. Having arrived in Jerusalem he would need wood from the king's forest for the walls, the doors and for his own residence. So he asked for these favors. The king graciously granted them all.

Nehemiah reduced the vision to a series of jobs, each to be done within a reasonable time. This is an essential step in the implementation of a vision. There can be no progress until it happens. Every good work exists first in the mind of a leader before it becomes reality. One wonders how many visions have died with the people who received them because those who had the visions were unable or unwilling to do the hard work of bringing the vision to fulfillment.

Some leaders need help in the planning process. Moses, for example, one of the world's greatest leaders, learned how to organize himself and his people to get work done from his father-in-law, Jethro. God gives different gifts to different people. Blessed is the leader who recognizes this and who will then, humbly, receive help from others. If a leader reaches out for help it should not be seen as a sign of weakness but of strength. After all, who has all the gifts? As leaders open themselves to the ministry of the other gifts in the brotherhood, they advance the work of the Kingdom mightily. A leader need not do all of the planning, yet he must assure that the planning gets done. The vision must become a living reality.

Think About It

Should a leader be likened to the coach of a sports team, or to one of the players? To the referee or the owner of the team? Should leaders be the visionaries or the planners? Are both elements being used in the church? Which is the most important, vision or planning? How do planners catch the vision?

14

Personal Disciplines:
Growing in Courage

When Sanballat . . . and Tobiah . . . heard about this, they were very much disturbed that someone had come to promote the welfare of the Israelites.

—Nehemiah 2:10

When Sanballet, Tobiah, the Arabs, the Ammonites and the men of Ashdod heard that the repairs to Jerusalem's walls had gone ahead and that the gaps were being closed, they were very angry. They plotted against it. But we prayed to our God and posted a guard day and night to meet this threat.

—Nehemiah 4:7-8

The courage which Nehemiah exhibited in his life was quite unbelievable from a human point of view. He encountered difficulties which would have paralyzed most of us. Not only did he need to overcome doubts within himself, but he had to confront the opponents of the vision from without.

Sometimes bringing a vision to reality requires all of our courage. Christian leaders will encounter all sorts of opposition to God's work. In Nehemiah's case, Sanballat (which literally means "sin gives life"), Tobiah and others were profiting from Jerusalem's miserable condition, so they tried to thwart Nehemiah's effort at every juncture.

Where did Nehemiah get such phenomenal courage? It was certainly not based on his belief that he would find no opposition. He found persistent, stubborn opposition.

Nor was it based on his belief that he was capable of doing the job that was at hand. To be sure, he had succeeded in getting King Artexerxes' support, but that was only one small victory. He faced what looked like insurmountable difficulties after that. Sanballat and his cronies were a hard lot.

We might ask, why should Nehemiah leave a job in which he was highly successful to step out in faith to try something which only a "fool" would try? In any case, what did he know about building walls and setting doors? To be sure, he knew very little. He had to face the possibility of failing, of making a fool of himself.

Nehemiah's courage was the direct result of God's spirit at work within him. He was prompted by the vision, by a divine love and by the assurance that what God calls people to do he will enable them to do.

True Christian courage does not arise from self-confidence. In fact, it is often quite the contrary. Moses had convinced himself that he should not do what God wanted him to do. Yet after God empowered him for this work, he walked into Pharoah's presence with striking boldness. The secret was that in his weakness Moses provided God with an opportunity to work. God's power works best through weakness. In fact, one of the hindrances to God's ministry in the world is our conviction that we can do things without him.

When Jesus asked the disciples if they could drink the cup of suffering he was about to drink, they replied with "self" confidence, "We can" (Mark 10:39). Before long they were scattered and fearful. They lost their courage.

However, a few days later after receiving the infilling of the Holy Spirit at Pentecost, all that changed for the disciples. They became courageous witnesses to the Gospel, even though they were beaten and persecuted.

A Christian leader's courage must be based on God's promises. The correct stance is, "I cannot. But the Lord can, and he is in me." If this is the case, a leader's courage has a sure foundation and is not simply courage based on human abilities or self-confidence. Leaders are usually strong, highly motivated people with a goodly portion of self-assurance. It is not easy for them to stand in weakness before the cross of Jesus Christ, but his love cannot flow through them until they do so.

Think About It

What is the difference between courage and arrogance? Moses was very courageous, yet he was described as a meek man. How is that? What can congregations do to encourage leaders to be more courageous? What are some of the greatest hindrances to courage?

15

Social Disciplines:
Building Team

The God of heaven will give us success. We his servants will start rebuilding .
—Nehemiah 2:20

One of the reasons that Jerusalem's walls lay in ruins was that there had been no unity among the inhabitants. Each person or family was looking out for "Number One." No one bothered to look after the public good except Ezra, who had recently returned from exile, and a few others. This state of affairs would have gone on and on if it were not for the leadership of Nehemiah who took divergent groups and individuals and welded them into a work force. Even while they were working on the wall tensions surfaced, but Nehemiah nipped in the bud the incipient hostile feelings which were certainly there. The enemy works night and day to divide the workers. The struggle usually begins with a small thing such as, "Where does my wall end and the other fellow's begin?" *or* "How does my wall compare with his wall?" When such feelings are aroused, a leader must be very careful lest the whole business go up in flames. An effective leader works well as a member of the team and is able to do the work of a peacemaker. He refuses to encourage any divisive spirit in the group but rather seeks to be part of the solution.

Great leaders of biblical history worked well in team settings. Moses had Aaron and Miriam (Micah 6:4) as his partners, David had Ahithophel, Jesus had the twelve, Paul worked with Barnabas, Silas, Timothy and Luke. Our spirituality is purified as we rub shoulders with other brothers and sisters on our team. Nehemiah, even though he was a very strong person and the one who had received the vision, determined to work on a team and did so with remarkable grace.

Not only was Nehemiah a good team worker, he was also tolerant of the shortcomings of others. He did not insist on having only professional stone masons and carpenters to build the wall. He took whoever was available and put them to work. Have you ever noted the kinds of people who took to the heavy task of wall building? They included the high priest and his fellow priests, a goldsmith, a perfume maker, the ruler of the half-district, Shallum and his daughters, Levites, temple servants, the guard at the East Gate merchants. Not one mason is named! Nehemiah learned to accept what was there and to utilize it. This is a lesson all Christian leaders should learn. It is never helpful to wish for what we do not have. We discover that if we use what is at hand, we are utterly amazed at what God can do.

Not only did Nehemiah understand the limitations of his workers, he also knew that everyone would not work with the same enthusiasm or even with the same motivation.

Some did enthusiastic work like Baruch. Some did ordinary work. Some did careful work like the sons of

Hassenaah, who in rebuilding the Fish Gate laid its beams, put its doors and bolts and bars in place. Some did work which benefited them, like the several who repaired "each in front of his own house". Some did double work. Others did monumental tasks, like Hanun and the residents at Zanoah who, after completing the Valley Gate, also repaired five hundred yards of the wall. But unfortunately, there were some who did not join in. "As for you, you have no share in Jerusalem or any claim or historic right to it" (Neh. 2:20). Good work, Nehemiah!

A good leader does not demand equal work or commitment from everyone but encourages all to do their best. He does not spend all of his time trying to harness the reluctant or recalcitrant ones. Neither does he fail to give credit to those who do exemplary work. Was it not gracious of Nehemiah to write down the names of those people and what they did? Their names still stand in the holy record while the walls of Jerusalem which they built have been destroyed long since.

The effects of disunity are devastating, we all know that. Disunity can bring work to a halt. Because the workers were separated from each other on the wall, Nehemiah realized that the enemy could easily penetrate their ranks. He told the nobles, the rulers and the rest of the people, "The work is extensive and spread out and we are widely separated from each other along the wall" (4:19). Nehemiah decided to consolidate them on the wall so that they would form a complete circle of resistance. In the same way, we dare not allow our work to separate us. When we get separated on the wall, we must find one another again and join our efforts in love. This is especially important for leaders because the enemy of our souls seeks to destroy unity among the leaders.

As a boy, when our large family went to town Dad said, "We'll meet at the clock." As Christians we meet, not at the clock, but at the cross of Calvary where Jesus' blood is spilled. There we find one another, and our mutual love is restored.

Think About It

How important is love in the ministry of a congregation? Is there a way for persons in your congregation to express themselves freely without feeling out of place? Is there an opportunity to express forgiveness and repentance? What should the leaders do to make every member feel absolutely at home in the congregation?

16

Social Disciplines:
Foreseeing Trouble

When Sanballat heard that we were rebuilding the wall, he became angry and was greatly incensed" (Nehemiah 4:1). "Hear us, O God, for we are despised.

—Nehemiah 4:4

So we continued the work with half the men holding spears, from the first light of dawn till the stars came out. . . . Neither I nor my brothers nor my men nor the guards with me took off our clothes; each had his weapon, even when we went for water.

—Nehemiah 4:21, 23

An effective Christian leader knows that a spiritual battle is raging. Furthermore, he knows that when Satan's kingdom is invaded or threatened in any way, the enemy stirs himself and fights back violently. When God's people confront Satan they are engaged in a cosmic struggle. It is a "hot" war.

Nehemiah had three very cunning enemies—
Sanballat, Tobiah, and Geshem, who set about to
frustrate his good work. In addition they enlisted the
support of the Arabs, the Ammonites and the men of
Ashdod (4:7). "They all plotted together to fight against
Jerusalem and to stir up trouble against it" (4:8). Satan
brought together a powerful combination of all evil
forces to frustrate the people of God in Jerusalem. And
he continues this work today. Where God works the
enemy also works, desperately.

Paul tells us (Eph. 3:10) that our battle is not against
flesh and blood but against the principalities and the
powers in heavenly places. When Nehemiah's enemies
saw that the breaches were being filled they were
enraged (Neh. 4:7). They vented their wrath and their
scorn on the builders of the wall. "They plotted together
to come and fight against Jerusalem and stir up trouble
against it" (4:8). Through prayer Nehemiah thwarted the
enemies' plans that day, but they returned again and
again. They tried to frustrate the good work at every
stage. As the wall was going up, they used ridicule and
sarcasm.

Notice the tricks of the devil. First, he told the truth,
at least in part. No one knew better than the builders
that their wall was not as good as it should have been.
After all, those workers had no experience at all in
building walls. So the enemies were not far off the mark
when they said, "What they are building—if even a fox
climbed up on it, he would break down their walls of
stones" (4:3). That was an exaggeration, but in a way they
were right. It was not a very strong wall. The enemy
sometimes tells the truth just to discourage us. We must
learn to discern the evil intent which lurks behind his
attacks.

Secondly, the enemy tried to bring division among
the workers. When the workers were widely separated

on the wall, the enemy planted discord, fear and confusion among them to frustrate their efforts.

Thirdly, Satan brought discouragement, knowing that the builder's strength was giving out. "Will they finish in a day?" the scoffers asked. Then, too, the builders said, "There is so much rubble that we cannot rebuild the wall" (4:10). Discouragement opens the door for the enemy to simply walk in.

Fourthly, the enemies instilled fear. They said, "Before they know it or see us, we will be right there among them and will kill them and put an end to the work" (4:11). When this news reached the ears of the workers, they were paralyzed. They could find no release from their disabling fear. Nehemiah wrote, "The Jews who were near them [the enemies] came and told us *ten times over*, `Wherever you turn, they will attack us'" (4:12).

Things were getting desperate. Just when the work was half finished (4:6) the whole project was placed in jeopardy by the enemy. The people were losing heart because of fear and unbelief. Now, what to do? It is exactly at this point that most good works of mercy fail. After initial exhilaration is over, frictions occur and doubts emerge about the ability of the leaders to bring the work to completion. All kinds of temptations accompany fatigue. Nehemiah, bless him, realized the crucial importance of this moment. He and his fellow leaders immediately gave themselves to prayer (4:9). Before prayer, however, he set a guard day and night to be on the lookout for trouble. While in prayer they received the confirming word from the Lord to go on. The leaders stood among the people and said, "Don't be afraid of them. Remember the Lord, who is great and awesome, and fight for your brothers, your sons and your daughters, your wives and your homes" (4:14). "Our God will fight for us!" (4:20).

Furthermore, they developed a system whereby some performed guard duty while others proceeded with the construction of the wall. Their faith was renewed; their strength returned. Courage banished fear as they turned to God for aid. Then as they fastened their eyes on the growing walls rather than on the heaps of rubble, the work went forward. And so the wall was built, but the enemy was never very far off.

The apostle Paul explained the full Christian defense against the devil (Eph. 6). We have, as we already noted, the belt of truth on which all other defenses hang. It also protects our most vital organs. We have the breastplate of right living and the shoes of the Gospel of peace. We are also told to take the shield of faith and the helmet of salvation. Thus clad, we do battle with the enemy, assured of victory in the name of Christ. But always, the leader must be first to don the battle dress and the first to rush into the battle. Nehemiah was such a leader. Jesus Christ defeated the enemy with a glorious victory (Eph. 4:8). We have no option. Now the battle is ours to fight in the name and power of Jesus Christ.

Think About It

Can you recall any good efforts which were frustrated part way through by the tricks of the devil? What strategies does the enemy use in your situation? What are the strategies you can use to defeat the enemy? How can people get rid of their fears? How can leaders get rid of their fears?

17

Social Disciplines:
Leading People in Worship

Nehemiah said . . . , "This day is sacred to our Lord. Do not grieve, for the joy of the Lord is your strength."

—Nehemiah 8:10

The sound of rejoicing in Jerusalem could be heard far away.

—Nehemiah 12:43

Nehemiah could have come into Jerusalem preaching repentance as Jonah did, but he did not. It was not that the residents of Jerusalem did not need the message of repentance. They surely did. In fact God allowed Nebuchadnezzer to take Judah captive because they were ungodly and unrepentant. For this reason, God led his people into exile, but even there they failed to fully grasp the necessity of true repentance. When they returned to Jerusalem they seemed to have learned nothing. They continued to live compromised lives. Jerusalem's fundamental need, if we look at the situation honestly, was not the need for a stone wall to keep the enemies out, even though that was very important. Their need was much deeper than that. They needed to deal with the enemy which dwelt within, their sin against one another. They needed to have their sins forgiven so that they could forgive one another and get on with building the community of faith in Jerusalem. Nehemiah realized that, but the inhabitants first had to see the mighty hand of God at work in the successful rebuilding of the wall. Having seen this, they were then ready to take the great step of renewing their covenant with God, a renewal possible only through heart- searching repentance.

When the book of Nehemiah opens we see this great man repenting of sins, both his and those of his fathers, with mourning and fasting. Through repentance, his spirit was cleansed, his relationship with God was restored, he was able to accept God's vision for his people as his very own. Into that broken, contrite heart God poured his love, his grace and his power. It spelled an exciting new beginning for Nehemiah and, in turn, for the dispirited dwellers in Jerusalem.

Nehemiah must have longed and prayed for the day when all Jerusalem would fall on their knees before God, repenting of their sins just as he had done. After the wall was built the Word of God was preached and it happened. There they were, "fasting and wearing sackcloth and having dust on their heads. . . . They stood in their places and confessed their sins and the wickedness of their fathers" (9:1,2). That evening marked a new day for Jerusalem. Their repentance was much more significant than the dedication of the wall, even though the wall was a great accomplishment in its own right. The purpose for the exile was not fulfilled when the wall was built. Jerusalem had had a wall before the exile, for that matter, and within that strong wall the Children of Israel had displeased God. The purpose of the exile was to bring the nation to repentance. God needed a humbled, purified people for the coming of the Prince of Peace, Jesus Christ of Nazareth. When they opened their hearts in repentant faith, the blessing was, in a way, complete.

There are many leaders who can organize projects and see them through to completion, but there are precious few who can lead people into God's presence where people's hearts are broken and where they can be touched with the divine flame. What, one might rightly ask, is the purpose of a wall if the people who live within that wall turn their backs on God? They will not even be able to keep it in repair. They can fight one another inside a wall just as easily as they can without a wall. New walls do not make new communities; repentance, covenants and love do that.

The culmination of Nehemiah's vision occurred on that day when the inhabitants of Jerusalem renewed in writing their covenant with God. The leaders went forward one after the other and signed the covenant. At the very top of the list was the name of Nehemiah (10:1). He took the lead in putting himself on the line for God.

It is probably not very helpful to ask the question, "Should Christians be more concerned about spiritual problems than economic or social issues?" Servants of Jesus Christ must be concerned about both because Jesus was concerned about both. The legitimate question is, "What do these people, created in God's image, need?"

In reality, it is impossible to separate our spiritual need from other needs, including material needs. It is a fallacy to divide people up into spiritual and material compartments. True, only the soul remains for eternity; but as long as spirit, soul and body are together, they affect one another more than we know. The whole Gospel is for the whole person in his whole environment. A careful reading of Scripture will reveal that even nature, in some wonderful way, will be redeemed. God cares for the material aspects of life, and so should we.

We must practice what we preach, and we must preach what we practice.

The conclusion of the matter is that the work of witness is not complete until the people stand face-to-face with God and there repent of their sins so that they can love God with all their hearts and serve him in joy forever. Effective Christian leaders usher people into the presence of God where people must make decisions about their destiny.

Think About It

What are the problems that might emerge if people's physical needs are addressed first? Some people say, "Get people right with God and then their physical needs will be met." Is this true? What is the Christian response to physical need? What are some of the walls that need to be rebuilt in your own immediate community? How do you propose it should be done? What are some dangers that you must be aware of?

18

Social Disciplines:
Building Covenants

"Although we are of the same flesh and blood as our countrymen and though our sons are as good as theirs, yet we have to subject our sons and daughters to slavery. Some of our daughters have already been enslaved, but we are powerless, because our fields and our vineyards belong to others."

When I heard their outcry and these charges, I was very angry. . . . I told them . . . , "What you are doing is not right. Shouldn't you walk in the fear of our God to avoid the reproach of our Gentile enemies?"

—Nehemiah 5:5-6,9

When the impressive wall was finally finished, Nehemiah turned his attention to the persistent, ugly social problems in the city. That section of society which controlled most of the wealth took advantage of their brothers' weakness. Through the process of lending money at high rates of interest, they managed to set repayment requirements so high that families defaulted one after the other. Some poor families had to sell their sons and daughters into slavery to avoid being put to death. And these were *all Jews*. They shared the common blood of Abraham. It was a lamentable state of affairs. It seems impossible that brothers and sisters, not only in faith but in race and blood, could destroy one another like this. But they did. They disobeyed the law of God a thousand times over.

And the leaders just stood by and let it happen. Is it possible that the rulers themselves were benefiting from this dehumanizing practice? Is it possible that Sanballat and his kind who were so negative toward Nehemiah's work were motivated by selfish greed? History is full of such.

Nehemiah, a leader called by God to speak the Word of God among the people, exposed this unjust economic system for what it was, a way of keeping power in the hands of those who already had great power. The poor suffered terribly. Nehemiah took a mighty risk when he spoke out. But he did so, and the spirit of the Lord convicted the people. They repented, cried out for forgiveness, and God forgave them.

Their repentance went further than that. They agreed in writing that, "Every seventh year we will forego working the land and will cancel all debts" (10:31). Nehemiah was the first person to take pen in hand and sign the covenant. History does not tell us whether they adhered to this resolution. Hopefully many did. It is not enough to simply repent of evil; it is also necessary to make restitution. In this leaders must show the way.

A Christian leader must have a moral sense. He must be prepared to stand alone, if need be, for the sake of justice and right, particularly as it affects those whom he is responsible to shepherd. If the leader does not hate sin with a passionate hatred, he probably does not really love that which is good.

In the history of the Christian church many leaders began their ministries by humbly following Jesus in all of life. Then slowly they compromised themselves and in the course of time lost their moral uprightness. Revival cannot be sustained unless it goes on producing upright, God-fearing, ethical behavior. Revival is sustained by its own fruit—repentant faith toward God. God's people are called to live like Jesus, not simply pursue their own personal welfare at the expense of others.

Think About It

What are the greatest temptations threatening moral purity in your community? What is the stance of the Christian leaders with reference to this issue? Is it possible that some Christians exploit fellow Christians? How is this possible? Is the church as concerned about the morality of its members as it should be? Should the church set the standards of morality for an entire nation?

19

Social Disciplines:
Increasing Communal Joy

*At the dedication of the wall of Jerusalem, the
Levites were sought out from where they lived
and were brought to Jerusalem to celebrate
joyfully the dedication with songs of
thanksgiving and with the music of cymbals,
harps and lyres.*

—Nehemiah 12:27

I assigned two large choirs to give thanks
—Nehemiah 12:31

"The joy of the Lord is your strength."
—Nehemiah 8:10)

Nehemiah experienced the full range of human
emotion. We see him grieving for his sin as he poured
out his heart to God in the early part of the story. His
countenance was sad when he pondered the dreadful
state of his people in Jerusalem. These emotions were
not new to Nehemiah.

But sadness was not his only emotion. Follow him on to the day when the wall was dedicated. He assembled two huge choirs to sing songs of praise to God as they walked on the newly-built wall. One choir went one way on top of the wall and another choir went the other way. Nehemiah followed one of these choirs overjoyed by the privilege of being in the presence of God. When the two choirs met on the wall they descended into the house of God. Nehemiah wrote, "So did I." He rejoiced with the people, and he in turn was a model of thanksgiving. "On that day," Nehemiah recalled, "they offered great sacrifices, rejoicing because God had given them great joy. The women and children also rejoiced. The sound of rejoicing in Jerusalem could be heard far away" (Neh. 12:43).

This is the will of God, and the way of God's people. "I will rejoice in the Lord, I will be joyful in God my Savior" (Habakkuk 3:18). Joy is the unmistakable hallmark of the children of the Lord.

Too many Christian leaders seem to be so burdened with the great weight of leadership responsibilities that they have no joy, or at least that is the impression that they give. A truly great Christian leader carries his burdens with a joyful heart. This joyful heart is not the result of human achievement; it is based on the hope that God will achieve what he wants to achieve. For this reason, the Christian does not wait to rejoice until everything comes out right, but he rejoices even when the outcome is not clear.

The Psalmist said it so well, "Delight yourself in the Lord, and he will give you the desires of your heart" (Ps. 37:4). The delighting precedes all else.

Nehemiah was so convinced that joy and thanksgiving should mark God's people that he established a permanent village for singers who were paid by the nation. The singers did but one thing—they sang and brought gladness to the hearts of Israel. Singing is at the center of every spiritual revival. In the midst of perplexing problems, Christians sing. Singing may be the most convincing sign of Christian hope. Happy is the leader in whose heart there is a divine melody. It will show on his face and in his every attitude.

Think About It

What is the basis of your joy? How can a leader exhibit a joyful heart when things are going wrong? What did Nehemiah mean when he reminded the Jews, "The joy of the Lord is your strength?" (Neh. 8:10). What are the most persistent enemies of joy? How can those enemies be subdued?

20

Management Disciplines:
Preparing & Studying

I went out through the Valley Gate toward the Jackal Well and the Dung Gate, examining the walls of Jerusalem. . . . I went up the valley by night, examining the wall.
—Nehemiah 2:13-15

We all know that times are changing. We know that new questions arise in our changing societies. But are we aware of these changes and have we examined them carefully? An alert leader takes the time and trouble to discover what is actually happening, and he will not simply take things for granted. He ponders everything that touches the lives of his people.

Nehemiah's relatives were able to give him a general idea of the condition of the walls, but he needed to know how much material had to be found outside Jerusalem, the overall conditions, and so on. He was constantly collecting information, just like any good leader.

When Nehemiah got serious about examining the walls, he took a few people with him who had a comprehensive understanding of the situation. They could answer his questions and show him things which he might not otherwise have seen. We need the help of others in our research and understanding. Nehemiah took others with him so that there was more than one set of eyes that examined Jerusalem. These eyes could see for one another.

It is vitally important that leaders understand the situation in which God has placed them. Many leaders received their training outside of the area in which they now serve. It is doubly important for such leaders to understand *local* problems and the factors that have converged to create those problems. Only as leaders address the local situation will they be able to bring the Gospel to bear upon the actual world in which people live.

Leaders should be acquainted with what is going on in the local economic, educational, political and social arenas. They are responsible to keep up with the changing environment.

This means that leaders must go out of their way to find out what is happening, for example, among the youth, among the women, among those who control business and labor. All of these factors affect the lives of the people in the congregations. A leader should know at least ten percent more than his people about current trends sweeping through their society.

Think About It

A Christian leader should have the newspaper in one hand and the Bible in the other. What do you think this means? How should leaders guard against the temptation to not pay attention to new ideas and information? Why do some leaders fear new ideas?

How can a leader make sure that he is hearing from all of the people he is expected to lead?

21

Management Disciplines:
Keeping Positive

Then I said to them, "You see the trouble we are in: Jerusalem lies in ruins, and its gates have been burned with fire. Come, let us rebuild the wall of Jerusalem, and we will no longer be in disgrace."

—Nehemiah 2:17

Nehemiah saw much which had gone wrong. Things were not good at all. From east to west and from north to south the situation in Jerusalem was deplorable. It was a sight desperate enough to discourage the most optimistic spirit.

But Nehemiah was not crushed. He saw not only the destruction but the possibilities as well. Indeed there was a lot of rubble; but, to his delight, some sections of the wall needed only minor repairs and others, none. All was not lost. Here was a section that had not been destroyed. There was a beam which was as strong as the day it was put in place. Nehemiah saw it all.

Many people are so overwhelmed by the bad which seems to dominate a situation that they fail to see that which is still good. If our main objective is to see what is wrong, we will find enough to satisfy us because there is always plenty that is wrong in every situation. By concentrating on what has been broken, we too often overlook that which is strong.

We must have the orientation of Nehemiah. We do not close our eyes to the problems, but we have the eye of the Spirit to see that much good remains. The enemy discourages us with the destruction. Jesus, on the other hand, encourages us by showing us that not all is lost. As human beings we tend to concentrate on the bad news. Jesus helps us to recognize the good things which are happening as well. Even amid the rubble there is hope.

The negative leader will contaminate others with his negative feelings while the hopeful leader will encourage others to believe. Nothing kills the spirit of hope in a congregation more quickly or more thoroughly than the constant fault-finding of leaders. People are well aware of their deficiencies, and the last thing they need is to be constantly bombarded with a barrage of "you are terrible people" preaching. All is not lost. We know that, but sometimes it is hard to affirm what is good and build on it. This does not mean turning a blind eye to the faults; they are real. But constant criticism can be devastating.

Jesus saw so much evil in Israel. Even the temple which had been set aside for prayer had become a den of robbers. Jesus saw right through the hypocrisy of the religious rulers; they reminded him of whitewashed mausoleums, nice on the outside but foul on the inside. Jesus did not hesitate to expose these evils. But he did not stop there. He saw faith in unexpected places, and he built on the basis of that faith. In fact, he gave his life, not because all was hopeless, but because he knew hope was there.

Leaders set the tone for the people. Let that tone be such that people will be encouraged to think on "whatever is true, whatever is noble, whatever is right, whatever is pure, whatever is lovely, whatever is admirable" (Phil. 4:8). With such attitudes the Kingdom of God is built in joy and unity.

Think About It

Make a list of what is wrong in your congregation or denomination and another of what is right. You will probably find it easier to do the first than the second because the bad is what we usually talk about. Why not determine today to concentrate on the good in others not only for your own spiritual health, but also to encourage the brothers and sisters. You will be amazed at how eager people are for the least bit of affirmation. Name a Barnabas (son of consolation) around you. How important is he to the work of the Lord?

22

Management Disciplines:
Inspiring Others

I also told them about the gracious hand of my God upon me and what the king had said to me. They replied, "Let us start rebuilding." So they began this good work.

—Nehemiah 2:18

Nehemiah had the gift of inspiring others. Some people refer to this quality as "charisma." Not everyone has received a vision directly from God. Those people must be inspired by the person who received the vision in a way that helps others catch the vision just as he did. The people must ultimately do the work, so they must own the vision.

Nehemiah began with a few men and then, when the time was appropriate, he shared the vision with the priests, rulers, nobles and the potential workers. When they heard his words, they not only recognized that the vision was authentic, but they realized that they could participate in the vision as though it were their very own. Nehemiah was able to share the vision in such a winsome way that it became theirs. This common vision set the scene for the release of unbelievable energy.

We see an amazing thing here. Jerusalem's problem, when Nehemiah arrived on the scene, was the same as it had been for decades. The people were the very same people, and the broken walls lay in ruin as they had for many years. Everything was already there to get the job done, but the job was not getting done. One thing was missing: effective, God-honoring leadership. When that essential ingredient appeared on the scene, remarkable things began to happen. And so it is everywhere in the world.

God, in his foreknowledge, assures that the gifts are there among his people for the extension of the Kingdom and for the nurture of the saints. Jesus Christ measures out carefully the ingredients needed for the finished product (Eph. 4). These gifts are present in each Christian community, often lying dormant. What is required to bring it all together is God-inspired and Christ-honoring leadership. In "bodily" language, members must have a head. Jesus Christ is the Head; we know that. But as we read the Scriptures we discover that through the miracle of the new birth and the ministry of the Holy Spirit, the mind of Christ is formed in the mind of believers so that they begin to be concerned with that which concerns Christ. They serve as vessels through whom the divine will can flow. Leaders who have the mind of Christ (Phil. 3) within them make a world of difference.

Think About It

How does a leader allow the mind of Christ to operate in him? Do you know of leaders who lead with their own intelligence and strength? What will come of their ministry? What responsibility does the congregation have to assure that its leaders are conforming their minds to the mind of Christ? What pictures describe an effective Christian leader? A shepherd? An orchestra conductor? A doctor in charge a hospital? An army general? Think about it.

23

Management Disciplines:
Delegating Responsibility

I had said nothing to the Jews or priests or nobles or officials or any others who would be doing the work.

—Nehemiah 2:16

So we rebuilt the wall till all of it reached half its height, for the people worked with all their heart.

—Nehemiah 4:6

God told Nehemiah to build the wall. That became his responsibility. Now, how was he going to go about it? He could have decided to teach by example in which case he would have rolled up his sleeves and set to work laying stone upon stone. Then slowly others would have been put to shame for not helping, or they would have had pity on the weary fellow and helped him. In either case, it is doubtful if the wall would ever have been built. Nehemiah did not go about it that way. As a matter of fact, as far as we know, Nehemiah never put a stone to the wall. He may have done so, but that was not important to record. It was not important to describe how much wall Nehemiah built but how much wall the people built.

Listen to the text, "Eliashib the high priest and his fellow priests went to work and rebuilt the Sheep Gate . . . the Fish Gate was rebuilt by the sons of Hassenaah . . . The Jeshenah Gate was repaired by Joiada and Meshullam . . . The Valley Gate was repaired by Hanun and the residents of Zanoah . . . " (Neh. 3). Nehemiah and the elders helped each group to find their particular place to work and encouraged them in their task. Not only that, but Nehemiah wrote it all down in a book which we now read with great pleasure and profit.

Many people with different gifts were working here and there toward the common goal: to rebuild the wall and the gates. Each felt that his or her job was significant. Not only was the work of each significant but vitally important for the success of the entire project because we know that a wall is only as strong as its weakest part. The enemy does not seek out the impregnable parts of the wall when to attacks, but he looks for the weakest spot and attacks there. So it was vitally important that each person did his work well.

This picture of Nehemiah working behind the scenes to inspire the whole assembly stands in contrast to what we see in many churches today where a few people do all the work and then complain that others do not care. In other cases, the pastor does almost everything, at least everything that is important.

I have heard the statement that the "normal" church is like a basketball game where there are ten players badly in need of rest and a thousand spectators who are badly in need of exercise. Sometimes that description fits our congregations.

In the growth and ministry of the church a great deal can be done if the leaders assure that every member is properly employed in meaningful work for the Lord. And the thought should never occur about who gets the credit.

Think About It

How do you deal with people who do not want to get involved in the work of the congregation? Is there a tactful way to help leaders to delegate responsibilities to others? Is it true that the gifts are there in each congregation for the congregation's ministries? When is it appropriate to go outside of the congregation to bring in people with specific gifts?

24

Management Disciplines:
Persisting

I sent him this reply: "Nothing like what you are saying is happening; you are just making it up out of your head." They were all trying to frighten us, thinking, "Their hands will get too weak for the work, and it will not be completed." But I prayed, "Now strengthen my hands."

—Nehemiah 6:8-9

A leader who is called of God to lead his people must keep an eye on the work at hand, but he must also keep another eye open to spot troubles that lie ahead. The people expect him to foresee trouble and to warn them, because if the enemy gets in among the people without his knowing it, woe to that group. It is the leader's responsibility to scan the horizon regularly to detect the enemy's intentions.

The most dangerous moment in our work for God is when things have settled down nicely, each one is doing his part, and good things are happening. People become aware of the progress they are making, and the project becomes an item of conversation. The leaders are praised, and the people are lifted up. In our time they would be written up in the press. At such times be careful. I once heard a friend say, "The devil reads the newspapers." When good things happen for God, the enemy brings in his big guns to wreck it all."

Leaders dare not be intimidated by the wrath of the enemy nor dare they get discouraged because the workers are beginning to slack off. Not at all. Leaders, if they are to fulfill the purpose of their gifting, must expose the enemy, point once again to the promises of God and then, along with the people, confront the enemy. By all means, leaders must never give up. No obstacle will come in their way that can defeat their Savior and Lord. Leaders must carry on in spite of the weariness of their people, and in spite of their own weariness.

the enemies of Nehemiah saw that the breaches were about to be closed, determined to stop the work then and there. They did so by striking fear hearts of the workers. The rubble became more obvious, and the people began to get weary; their energy flagged. A spokesman from Judah said, "The strength of the laborers is giving out, and there is so much rubble that we cannot rebuild the wall" (Neh. 4:10). The enemy ridiculed them ten times until their resolve weakened.

This is the way of the enemy. If he cannot stop a good work before it starts, he will cause people to abandon the vision part way through. Many worthy projects lie uncompleted because of obstacles and difficulties encountered part way through.

Nehemiah set watches all over the wall to keep the mocking enemies away; and after encouraging the people, the workers all returned to the wall and each took up the work which had been assigned to him (4:15).

Think About It

How is the enemy frustrating the work of God in your fellowships? Do the people encourage their leaders to warn them of impending dangers? If the leaders are not on their watch detecting the enemy's strategies, who in your fellowship is doing this? Describe the best way in your situation, to weaken the power of the enemy. At what point is a good work for God in greatest jeopardy? Have you ever known a Christian leader to give up? Why do you think that happened?

Conclusion

The book of Nehemiah is the last "historical book" of the Old Testament. It is significant that the last sentences of this great book were, "I purified the priests and the Levites of everything foreign, and assigned them duties, each his own task. I also made provision for contributions of wood at designated times, and for the first fruits. Remember me with favor, O my God" (13:30-31).

Nehemiah, in the end, submitted his own leadership to the gaze of divine scrutiny. He, like Paul, that great Apostle to the Nations, had not been unfaithful to the heavenly vision but had fixed his eyes on the heavenly calling every day of his ministry. In human terms there were successes and failures. God does not judge on that basis but on whether or not we are faithful to the heavenly vision. We are judged, not on our ability, but on our availability; not according to our works, but according to our openness to his grace.

Nehemiah concluded a life's work with the assurance that God who had called him and who had given him the vision was also the God who empowered and supported him to the end. He could rest assured on God's gracious favor. We can do the same!